Forewo

I first heard the phrase "First my daughter Sophie. I was co ....g about something insignificant and meaningless, and she said to me, "sounds like a First World Problem, Dad." That phrase sparked something in my mind to start writing down some of my random thoughts and small problems. While writing this book, I was going through a mid-life crisis, struggling with trying to figure out and understand my purpose in life. Writing these FWP's down helped me to put in perspective how good I really have it, and how some people who have almost nothing would give anything to be living in my shoes, even with my small problems. None of these FWP's are meant to make fun of or belittle anyone who is worse off than I am. They are more for us to see how the small irritations in our everyday lives get blown out of proportion. So when you think you are at your wit's end, just remember that there is somebody out there much worse off than you are.

First World Problems

When I started writing this book,

I was using a spiral notebook.

So my initial First World Problem (FWP)

has to do with what was just to my left.

Left-handed people hate spiral

notebooks.

Because when you start writing on the

right side of the notebook, your

hand has to rest on the spiral.

It's awkward and uncomfortable!

It's actually really hard to have
to think up first world problems,
so you can share them
with others just for a laugh.
It's time consuming, and quite
strenuous!

First and Third World Problem...

TRUMP!!!

I hate it when you've gone through the drive through window at a fast food restaurant, and when you start to eat your burger, you notice that the bun, meat, and cheese don't all line up with each other.

Messy!!!

Leaving the microwave popcorn in for 15 seconds too long. When some of the kernels burn, it makes the rest of the bag taste burnt!!!
Might as well just start all over.

When you're on a run and one of your shoe laces is tied tighter than the other one, you then have to stop, bend down, and tie it tighter. By then, your whole routine is thrown off!!!
Might as well just walk home!?!?

I hate it when you're flossing, and you get a piece of floss stuck in between your teeth. So now you have to get another piece just to get the first piece out. Wasteful!!!

It strains my mind when I'm at the

grocery store, having to choose

between 16

different types of Cheerios.

(I actually looked it up)

Don't you hate it when you take a load of clothes out of the dryer, and when you put one of the pairs of pants on, the hot button on your pants burns your stomach!!!

You pick up your smart phone, and as you start to enter your password, you accidentally double click one of the numbers. But, you don't know which one, so now you have to start all over and enter it again.

What a waste of time!!!

It's a cold snowy day. You're inside, with

a warm roaring fire,

working a jigsaw puzzle.

When you're almost finished with the

puzzle, you notice that one of the puzzle

pieces is missing.

It totally ruins the moment!

Life sucks!

Don't you hate it when you're on
vacation, and your hotel shower head is
so low that you have to bend down a bit
just to wash your hair. Not to mention
that the water pressure isn't
what you are used to.
So now you have to put up with this
for the next two weeks!
It might just ruin your entire trip!

I hate it when you're snacking on Jelly Belly jellybeans, and without paying attention, you accidently grab a butter flavored popcorn jellybean!

When you bite down on it, you immediately realize what a bad thing has just happened to you. The flavor stays in your mouth way too long!

When you're at a Colorado ski resort, and it's the last run of the day, one hour from your dinner reservations. Half way up the lift, the lift chair stops. While you are waiting for it to start up again, the bright sun beats down on you, and you start to get too hot.
Then you start thinking,
"this is just great, I'm going to be late for my dinner reservations!"
Can things get any worse?!?!

I hate it when Bed Bath and Beyond sends you a $5.00 off coupon, when you spend $15.00 or more.

So when you go to the store, and finally find what you want, it costs $14.99!

Is this some sort of sick "way up high on the corporate ladder" joke!?!?

Why can't someone make a microwave
that lets you leave the metal spoon in
the mug while it's heating up?
That way you don't have to set the
spoon down on the countertop.
It's messy.
I'm just saying.

I hate it when you get your next DVD from Netflix, and when you go to put it in your 5 disk DVD player, all 5 spots are full! Then you have to decide which one to take out to make room for your movie. Decisions, decisions...

I hate it when you wake up in the morning, and go to make a cup of coffee in your Keurig machine, but it's not turned on. So now you have to turn it on and wait for it to warm up. That is the longest minute and forty five seconds you will ever know!
(I actually timed it.)

This one really gets to me.

You drive to the bank to withdraw some

money from the drive through ATM.

When you enter $100.00, it gives it to

you in $20.00's, but they're all

stuck together. So now

you have to lick your

fingers to separate the bills.

What a royal pain!

It's irritating when you're new car shopping, and after looking at several dozen cars, you finally find the one that has all of the features you want, but it's not the right color. So when you spot a car that is the right color, it doesn't have all of the features you want. A person should never have to be faced with those kinds of sacrifices...ever!!!

I strongly dislike it when your shower caddy gets too gross to clean. So when you go to buy a new one, (probably $14.99 at Bed Bath and Beyond!), they don't have the same style as your old one. So reluctantly, you pick out a new one, fully knowing that you are going to have to arrange all of your products differently. So now you have to relearn where everything is.

Don't you hate it when you're going to the restroom, and when you have to put a new roll of toilet paper on the holder, you have to pick and peel, pick and peel, until 3 feet later you finally get it properly started. What a waste of toilet paper and time!

I really don't like it when you go to unload your dishwasher, but some time during the wash cycle, a cup got flipped right side up and filled up with dirty dish water. Now you have to carefully lift it out, dump it in the sink, and then put it back in the dishwasher to be re-cleaned. Really!?!?

I hate it when you come inside on a hot summer's day to get a drink of ice water, but as you're drinking it, danger is lurking right around the corner. The ice cubes have all stuck together, and have created an ice dam. Just as you notice what's about to happen, it's too late.
The ice cubes let loose, and water splashes your face and
goes down your front!
I bet the ice cube design people really get a kick out of that one!
They'll pay for it someday!!!

It's after 5:00pm on a Friday afternoon, and your toilet breaks. So you call a plumber, but they can't make it out there until Monday. Now you have to use the guest bathroom all weekend long! What an inconvenience!

It's late in the evening and you're hungry for a snack. So you decide to eat a bowl of cereal. You get a bowl and the cereal, but all of the tablespoons are in the dishwasher, still in the middle of the heat dry cycle. Now you're faced with a major dilemma:

1.) Do you use a teaspoon, which will make the cereal-to-milk ratio all wrong?

or

2.) Do you use a hot spoon that will warm the milk too fast with each bite? It's too late in the evening to have to make such a life-altering decision!

You're driving in your car on a hot summer's day, and even though the A/C is on, you feel a warmth coming from your seat. It's your seat heater!
It accidentally got turned on. Really?!?!
If your car seat can detect a small person sitting in it and automatically turn the air bag off, then surely it can detect that it's hot outside.

You're playing a game on your
smart phone, and in between rounds,
it automatically pauses and goes to an
advertisement that you are forced to
watch for 30 or more seconds. Well,
you could pass the time by turning your
Keurig machine on,
and waiting for it to warm up!

TUPPERWARE!!!

Where do I begin...

1.) Several of the lids are too close in size, so you have to sort through them all until you find the right numbered lid that matches the number on the container.

2.) With square Tupperware containers it is impossible to get all four corners to stay closed at the same time.

3.) Like the cup that gets turned right side up in the dishwasher, all Tupperware containers do this! You know, they're really not all that convenient!

I'm torn...

When doing the puzzles in the morning newspaper, I have to choose between two kinds of gel ink pens. The .05 or the .07. The thinner .05 makes nice neat lines, but tends to slightly tear through the paper if you apply too much pressure. The thicker .07, on the other hand, tends to blot a little too much if held down on the paper for too long. I sure wish they would make a .06! That would solve everything!

You're in the kitchen cooking dinner, and one of the steps to what you are making requires butter. So when you get the butter dish out, and take the lid off, there are crumbs on the butter from someone using it earlier that morning who was making toast. Now you have to take time away from making dinner and scrape the crumbs off of the butter! Where was that step in the recipe book?!?!

You decide to go out and see a movie.
You get to the theater, buy your tickets,
and get your refreshments,
but when you enter the theater,
all of the seats are taken,
except for the two all
the way down front and off to the left.
So now you have to watch the entire
movie looking up and to the right. You're
going to feel that one in the morning!
What a royal pain in the neck. (literally)

After eating a well prepared meal at
home, you feel something in between
your teeth with your tongue. So when
you get a toothpick, and start picking at
it for several minutes,
you still can't get it out.
I think it's time to improve the design of
the toothpick. Unless a caveman still
holds the patent!

I hate it when you're texting back and forth with a friend, and as you are typing a response to their text, they send another one through before you can respond to the first one. So now what do you do? Ignore the first one, and only respond to the second one, which might be considered rude? Or do you still keep typing, and respond to the first one? But now you're one text behind for the rest of the conversation. I just can't keep up with modern technology!

Wearing shorts on a hot summer's day...

Leather seats in your car that the sun

has been beating down on all day...

Do I really need

to finish this one for you?

If they can make seats that heat up in

the winter, surely they can make seats

that cool down in the summer.

My oldest son is in the USMC.

So when he comes

home on leave, we really enjoy the time

spent with him...but...this one is for

anyone who has a loved one in any

branch of the military. He'll start telling

us all about some of his many

experiences, which include way too

many acronyms. You don't want to be

rude and interrupt him just to have him

explain what he just said,

so you just smile and listen.

For example: PCCs and PCIs include

checking the EDL to include RCO7s,

PEQ16s and PVS24s. REALLY!!!

Well, at least it's good to see him.

Think about this one.

You need a new pair of cheater reading

glasses because your old ones are all

scratched up and foggy. But this is

where things go terribly wrong.

You have to take them off to look and

see what power level they are,

but you can't see it

because you just took them off!

So how on Earth did you ever buy them

in the first place?!?!

Like I mentioned earlier about the hotel

shower head being too low-- Well,

that just scratched the surface of

a multitude of hotel problems:

-Your card key never works

the first time you try it.

-Thin, coarse toilet paper.

-Having to read the Gideon Bible.

-Trying to figure out the little in-room

coffee maker.

-Not knowing any of the TV channels.

-The pillows are too firm.

-The wall A/C unit never

cools the room properly.

...the list goes on and on. So why even

bother going on a vacation?!?!

Have you ever tried opening a new box of cereal, but to open the inner liner, you need to be some sort of super hero. So as you are trying to pull it apart, it finally rips violently open, tearing one side of the liner! For the remainder of the box, you have to pour it from the side that's not torn. That means when you set the box down, it's not facing the way you're used to.

You are at your favorite sports bar,

and all of the 30+TVs

have every game on that

you could ever want to watch

...but a storm rolls through,

and knocks the signal out

to every TV!

So now what are we supposed to do?

Acknowledgements

I want to thank my lovely wife for coming up with a few FWP ideas, helping me edit my poor spelling, and getting my ideas into this book! Even with my good, though quirky sense of humor, she has laughed and put up with me the whole time. Also a thanks to my sister-in-law who helped with a few ideas of her own. Thanks to my brother and sister for either laughing their heads off because they thought my ideas were funny, or just laughing to be polite. My daughter and three boys usually roll their eyes at them, dispute them, and try to explain how to solve the problem. But deep down, I know they think they are truly funny. (not the kids, the FWP's)

11365206R00026

Printed in Great Britain
by Amazon